GREGORY
The Pigeon / Chicken

By
VALERIE OLSON

COPYRIGHT

Copyrights© 2024 Valerie Olson.
All rights reserved.
No part of this book may be reproduced, stored in a retrieval system, or transmitted in any form or by any means-electronic, mechanical, photocopy, recording, scanning, or other-except for brief quotations in critical reviews or articles, without the prior written permission of the publisher.

For inquiries, Email: info@americanbookpublisher.com Phone: (929)-563-6133
Website: www.americanbookpublisher.com

AUTHOR BIO

I am from a small town in central Idaho. I have lived on a working cattle ranch for the past 40+ years. I work at a local veterinary clinic and have always loved animals and telling stories to my children and grandchildren. Over the years I have been encouraged to start putting my stories into a book, so here I am today. This will be my first submission of one of my stories! Thank you

DEDICATION

Our family lives on a cattle ranch in the beautiful mountains of Salmon, Idaho.

I have cared for many different farm animals over the years and at one time had a farm petting zoo.

This book is based on a true story and inspired by all my grandchildren, who love my stories.

Thank you to my family and friends who encouraged me to make this book!

One day, while Gracie and Grayson were playing at their great-grandma Carole's house, they heard a small chirping noise.

When they decided to investigate where it was coming from, they spotted a small grey bird with downy yellow feathers poking out of its body. Their cousin Serenity had come to play as well. She said, "Let's see if we can catch him!" Never did they really think he would just sit on their grandma's flower pot and let them catch him,
but he did!

The little bird was afraid at first, but then realized the children were very nice and would not hurt him. They played all afternoon in the yard.

When they climbed up great-grandma's apple tree, the little bird hopped around in the grass, and he even flew up on the fence.

Instead of flying away, he waited for the children to finish playing.

When it was time to go home, all the children looked at each other and asked, "What shall we do with the bird?"

"Well," said Serenity, "first of all, I think he needs a name. Let's call him Gregory." "Yes," said Gracie, "I like that name. Let's call him Gregory!""

"I wonder what kind of bird he is," asked Grayson. "Let's go ask Uncle Doss. He will know.

Uncle Doss said Gregory was a baby pigeon who had just learned to fly. He must have wandered away from his mom and brothers and sisters.

Now he was all alone and was glad he had made new friends with the three children.

Gracie and Grayson asked their parents if they could take Gregory home to their house.

Mommy said, "But where would we keep him? We have three kitties that might try to eat him!"

So Serenity asked her grandma if she could take him home. Her grandma said, "We have nowhere to keep him that would be safe." The children were so sad but decided to turn him loose in the field. They turned to walk away, and when they looked back, guess who was following them to the car? Yes, Gregory!

Now, what were they going to do? "Let's ask Grandma Val if he can go live at her house.

She has lots of places for a pigeon to live." Grandma Val could never say no to her grandchildren, so it was settled. Gregory the pigeon would go live in her rabbit cage until he was older and could fly better.

Once Grandma Val got him settled in his new home, she gave him a bowl of water. He drank and drank more water. Poor Gregory was so thirsty! Gregory lived in the rabbit cage next to the chicken coop. Every day, he would hear them cackling when they laid their eggs and the roosters crowing early in the morning, but he could not see the chickens from his cage.

"I wonder what my new friends look like," asked Gregory. He would talk back to them and make a soft cooing noise. The chickens wondered who was talking to them from the rabbit cages, but they couldn't see him either.

One day, when Gracie and Grayson came over to play, Grandma Val said it was time to turn Gregory loose. Gracie caught him, and they carried him out to Grandpa's great big hay stack. She threw him into the air, and Grayson yelled, "Fly away, Gregory!"

He flew over to the fence and flapped his little wings as if he was waving goodbye. Everyone waved goodbye, thinking they would never see Gregory again.

Every day, Grandma Val would let her chickens out of the coop to free range. This meant they could wander around the ranch and peck at the grass and bugs.

They knew that come night, it was time to go back to their safe chicken coop and roost for the night. Grandma Val would go shut the door at dark so no skunks or raccoons would come into the chicken coop and try to eat the chickens!

One day, she went to let the chickens out of the coop, and guess who came running out the door?

Yes, it was Gregory! He had found his way back to the chickens and had decided to move in with them.

This was his new home, and the chickens seemed to accept him as one of their own. They had bonded when talking to each other when Gregory lived in the rabbit cage, even though they had never seen each other. The chickens accepted him into their home and shared their food and water with him.

Every night, he puts himself to bed in the chicken coop, where he knows he will be safe. Every morning, he runs out of the coop and pecks at the grass and even rolls in the dirt to dust himself, just like the chickens do. He thinks he is a chicken! Someday, he might meet another pigeon and decide to leave his chicken friends, but for now, he is very happy living with his chicken family.

THE END

Made in United States
Orlando, FL
11 June 2024